Construction Zone

Bulldozers

by Rebecca Pettiford

Bullfrog Books

Ideas for Parents and Teachers

Bullfrog Books let children practice reading informational text at the earliest reading levels. Repetition, familiar words, and photo labels support early readers.

Before Reading

- Discuss the cover photo. What does it tell them?
- Look at the picture glossary together. Read and discuss the words.

Read the Book

- "Walk" through the book and look at the photos. Let the child ask questions. Point out the photo labels.
- Read the book to the child, or have him or her read independently.

After Reading

- Prompt the child to think more. Ask: Bulldozers are big machines. They push and dig. Can you name other big machines that do this?

Bullfrog Books are published by Jump!
5357 Penn Avenue South
Minneapolis, MN 55419
www.jumplibrary.com

Library of Congress Cataloging-in-Publication Data

Names: Pettiford, Rebecca, author.
Title: Bulldozers / by Rebecca Pettiford.
Description: Minneapolis, MN: Jump!, Inc., [2023]
Series: Construction zone | Includes index.
Audience: Ages 5–8.
Identifiers: LCCN 2021048964 (print)
LCCN 2021048965 (ebook)
ISBN 9781636908465 (hardcover)
ISBN 9781636908472 (paperback)
ISBN 9781636908489 (ebook)
Subjects: LCSH: Bulldozers—Juvenile literature.
Earthwork—Juvenile literature.
Classification: LCC TA735 .P463 2023 (print)
LCC TA735 (ebook) | DDC 629.225—dc23/eng/20211122
LC record available at https://lccn.loc.gov/2021048964
LC ebook record available at https://lccn.loc.gov/2021048965

Editor: Jenna Gleisner
Designer: Michelle Sonnek
Content Consultant: Ryan Bauer

Photo Credits: kamski/Can Stock Photo, cover; Westermak/Shutterstock, 1; Vladimir Sazonov/Shutterstock, 3; VanderWolf Images/Shutterstock, 4; smereka/Shutterstock, 5; Editor77/Dreamstime, 6–7; Dan Leeth/Alamy, 8–9, 23tm; Praphan Jampala/Shutterstock, 10–11, 23br; Dmitry Kalinovsky/Shutterstock, 12, 23bm; Jozef_Culak/Shutterstock, 13; Juan Enrique del Barrio/Shutterstock, 14–15, 16–17, 23tl, 23tr; Aleksandar Blanusa/Shutterstock, 18; Mr Twister/Shutterstock, 19, 23bl; dnaveh/iStock, 20–21; Lampochka/iStock, 22; Art Konovalov/Shutterstock, 24.

Printed in the United States of America at Corporate Graphics in North Mankato, Minnesota.

Table of Contents

A Big Push

Bulldozers are big machines.

They push things.

A park will be built here.
A bulldozer helps.
It gets the land ready.

7

Kay drives the bulldozer.
She sits in the cab.

cab

track

The bulldozer moves on tracks.

They roll.

Kay lowers the ripper.

It looks like a claw.

ripper

It rips up the land.

blade

A blade is on the front.

It is big.

The blade pushes rocks.
It clears the land.

It pushes dirt.

It makes the land even.

The land is ready.

The park is finished.
The bulldozer helped!

Parts of a Bulldozer

What are the parts of a bulldozer? Take a look!

cab

ripper

track

blade

Picture Glossary

blade
The big, heavy part on the front of a bulldozer that pushes things.

cab
The area in a big machine where the driver sits.

clears
Removes things that are covering or blocking a place.

even
Flat and level.

ripper
The part on the back of a bulldozer that rips up land.

tracks
The steel belts on the bottom of a bulldozer that move the machine.

23

Index

To Learn More

Finding more information is as easy as 1, 2, 3.

❶ Go to www.factsurfer.com

❷ Enter "bulldozers" into the search box.

❸ Choose your book to see a list of websites.